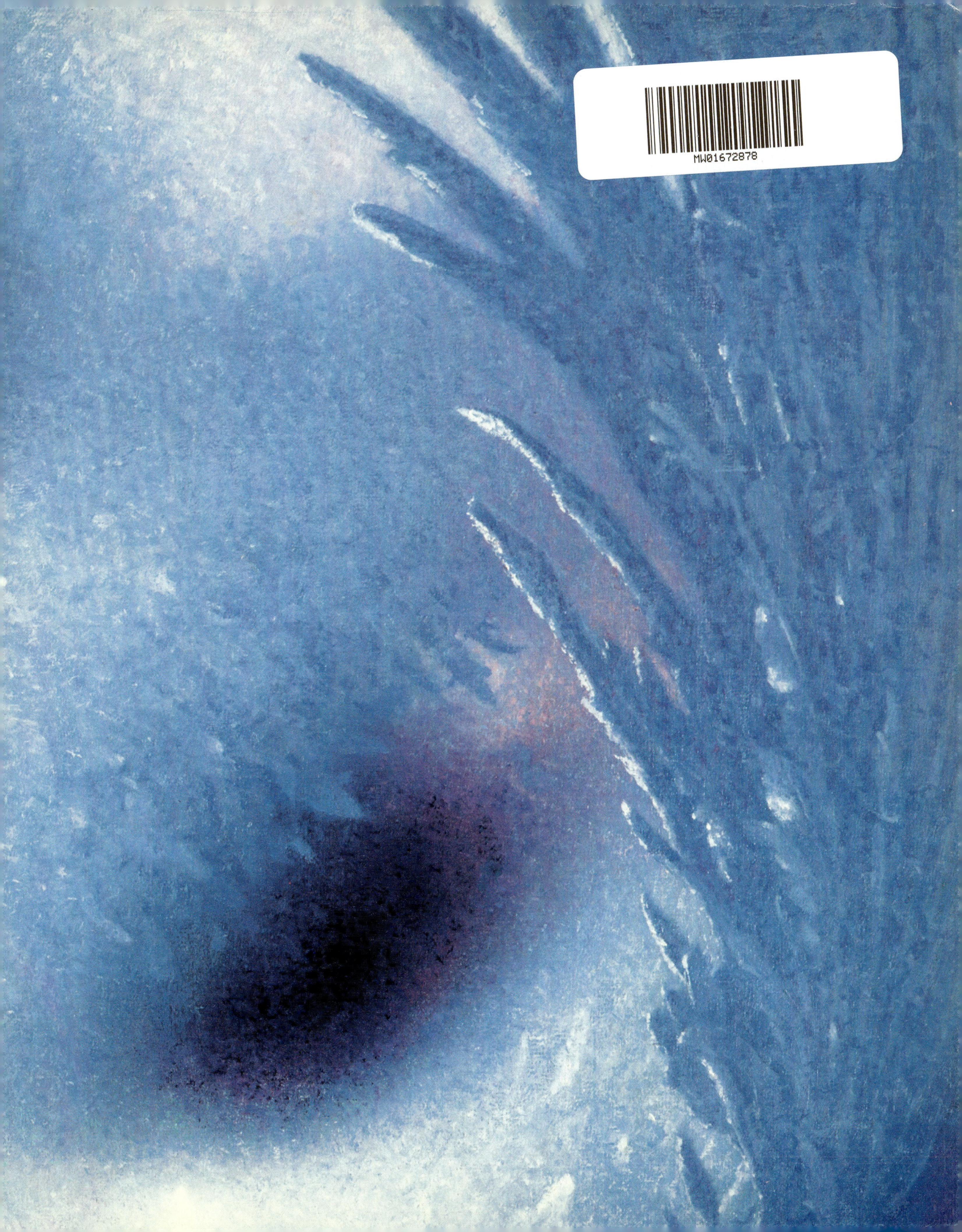

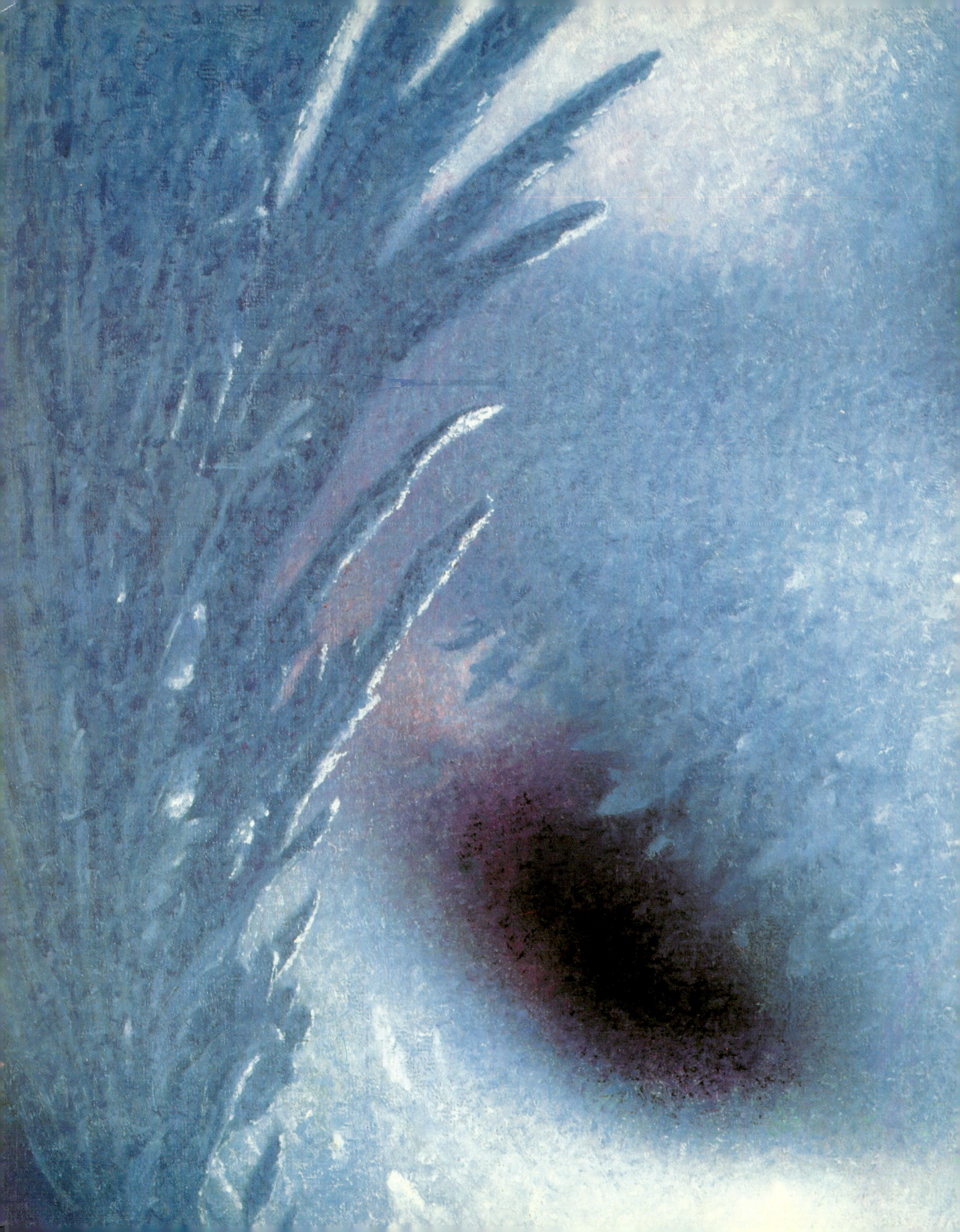

This Is the Star

For the newly born.
J.D.

To Lin.
G.B.

This Is the Star

JOYCE DUNBAR • GARY BLYTHE

SCHOLASTIC INC.
New York Toronto London Auckland Sydney

This is the star in the sky.

These are the shepherds watching by night
That saw the star in the sky.

This is the angel shining bright
Who came to the shepherds watching by night
That saw the star in the sky.

This is the donkey with precious load
Trudging the long and weary road,
Looked on by the angel shining bright
Who came to the shepherds watching by night
That saw the star in the sky.

This is the inn where the only room
Was a stable out in the lamplit gloom
For the donkey and his precious load
Who trudged the long and weary road,
Looked on by the angel shining bright
Who came to the shepherds watching by night
That saw the star in the sky.

This is the ox and this is the ass
Who saw such wonders come to pass
At the darkened inn where the only room
Was a stable out in the lamplit gloom
For the donkey and his precious load
Who trudged the long and weary road,
Looked on by the angel shining bright
Who came to the shepherds watching by night
That saw the star in the sky.

This is the manger warm with hay
Wherein a newborn baby lay.
This is the ox and this the ass
Who saw these wonders come to pass
At the darkened inn where the only room
Was a stable out in the lamplit gloom
For the donkey and his precious load
Who trudged the long and weary road,
Looked on by the angel shining bright
Who came to the shepherds watching by night
That saw the star in the sky.

This is the gold and fragrant myrrh
And frankincense, the gifts that were
Placed by the manger warm with hay
Wherein a newborn baby lay.
This is the ox and this the ass
Who saw these wonders come to pass
At the darkened inn where the only room
Was a stable out in the lamplit gloom
For the donkey and his precious load
Who trudged the long and weary road,
Looked on by the angel shining bright
Who came to the shepherds watching by night
That saw the star in the sky.

These are the wise men come from afar
Who also saw and followed the star,
Bearing the gold and fragrant myrrh
And frankincense, the gifts that were
Placed by the manger warm with hay
Wherein a newborn baby lay.
This is the ox and this the ass
Who saw these wonders come to pass
At the darkened inn where the only room
Was a stable out in the lamplit gloom
For the donkey and his precious load
Who trudged the long and weary road,
Looked on by the angel shining bright
Who came to the shepherds watching by night
That saw the star in the sky.

This is the child that was born.

This is the Christ child born to be king
While hosts of heavenly angels sing.
These are the wise men come from afar
Who also saw and followed the star,
Bearing the gold and fragrant myrrh
And frankincense, the gifts that were
Placed by the manger warm with hay
Wherein a newborn baby lay.
This is the ox and this the ass
Who saw these wonders come to pass
At the darkened inn where the only room
Was a stable out in the lamplit gloom
For the donkey and his precious load
Who trudged the long and weary road,
Looked on by the angel shining bright
Who came to the shepherds watching by night
That saw the star in the sky.

Still shines the star in the sky.

ISBN 0-590-38174-1

 Published by Scholastic Inc., 555 Broadway, New York, NY 10012, by arrangement with Harcourt Brace & Company.

12 11 10 9 8 7 6 5 4 7 8 9/9 0 1 2/0

Printed in the U.S.A. 08
First Scholastic printing, November 1997

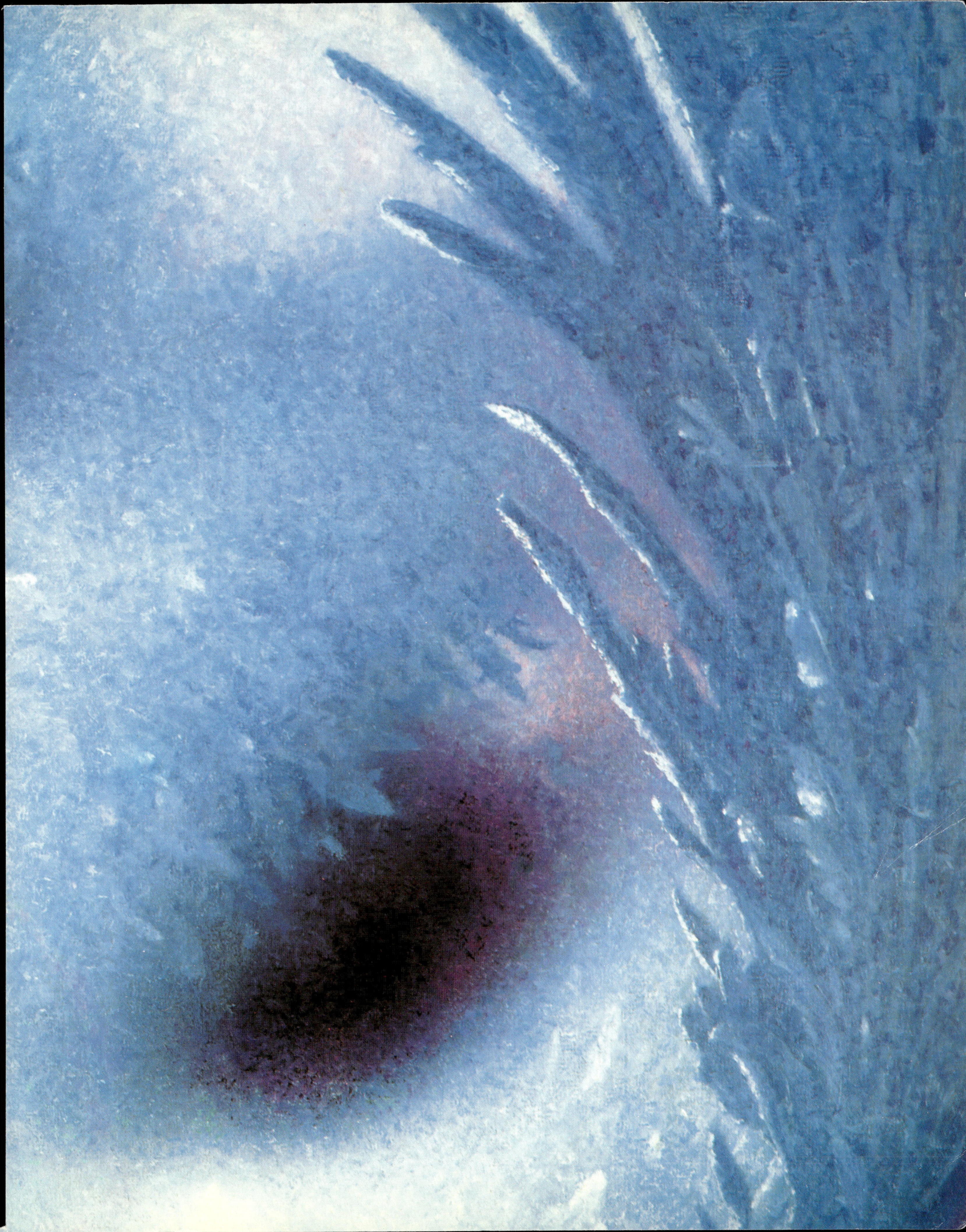

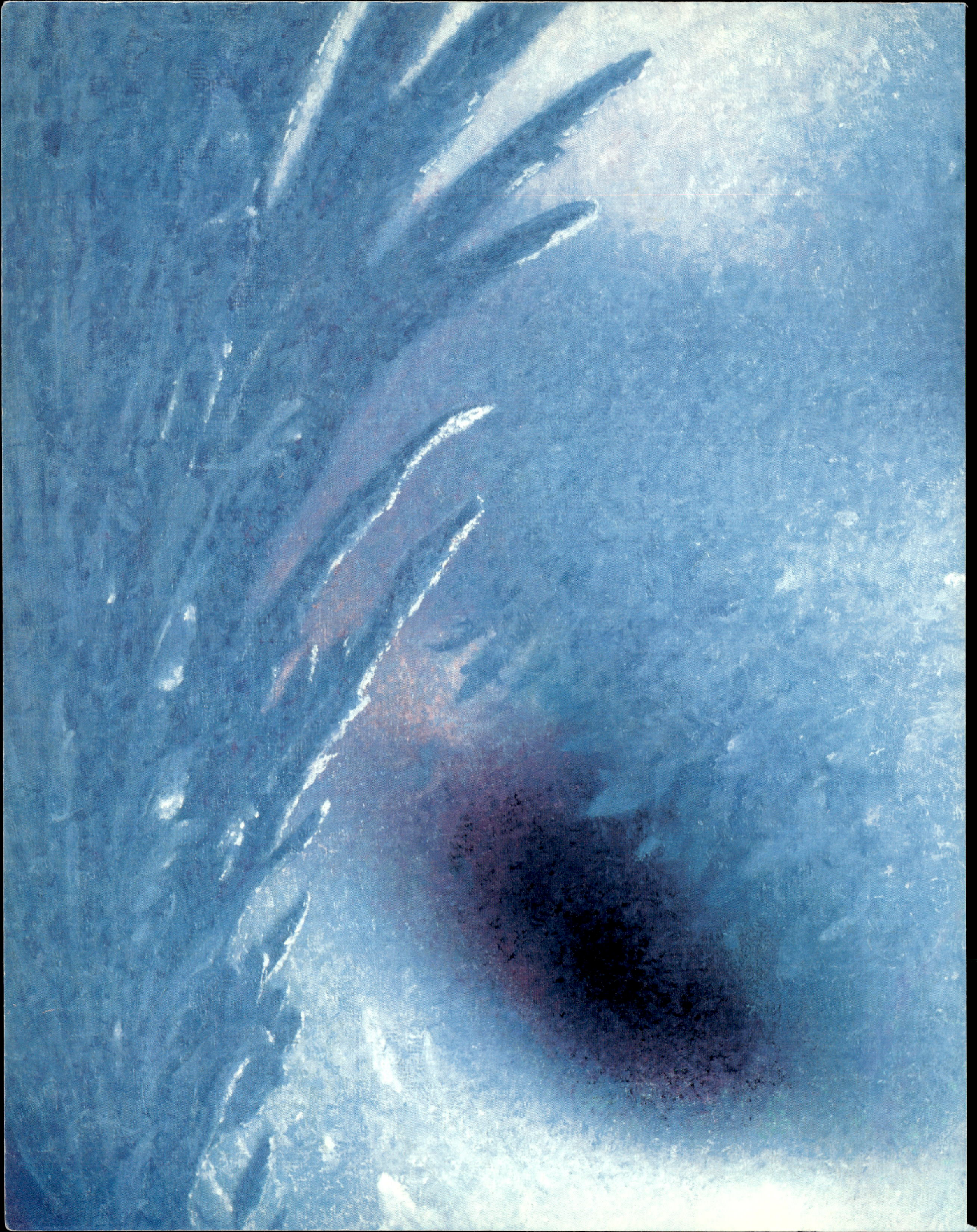

NATIONAL GEOGRAPHIC LEARNING | CENGAGE

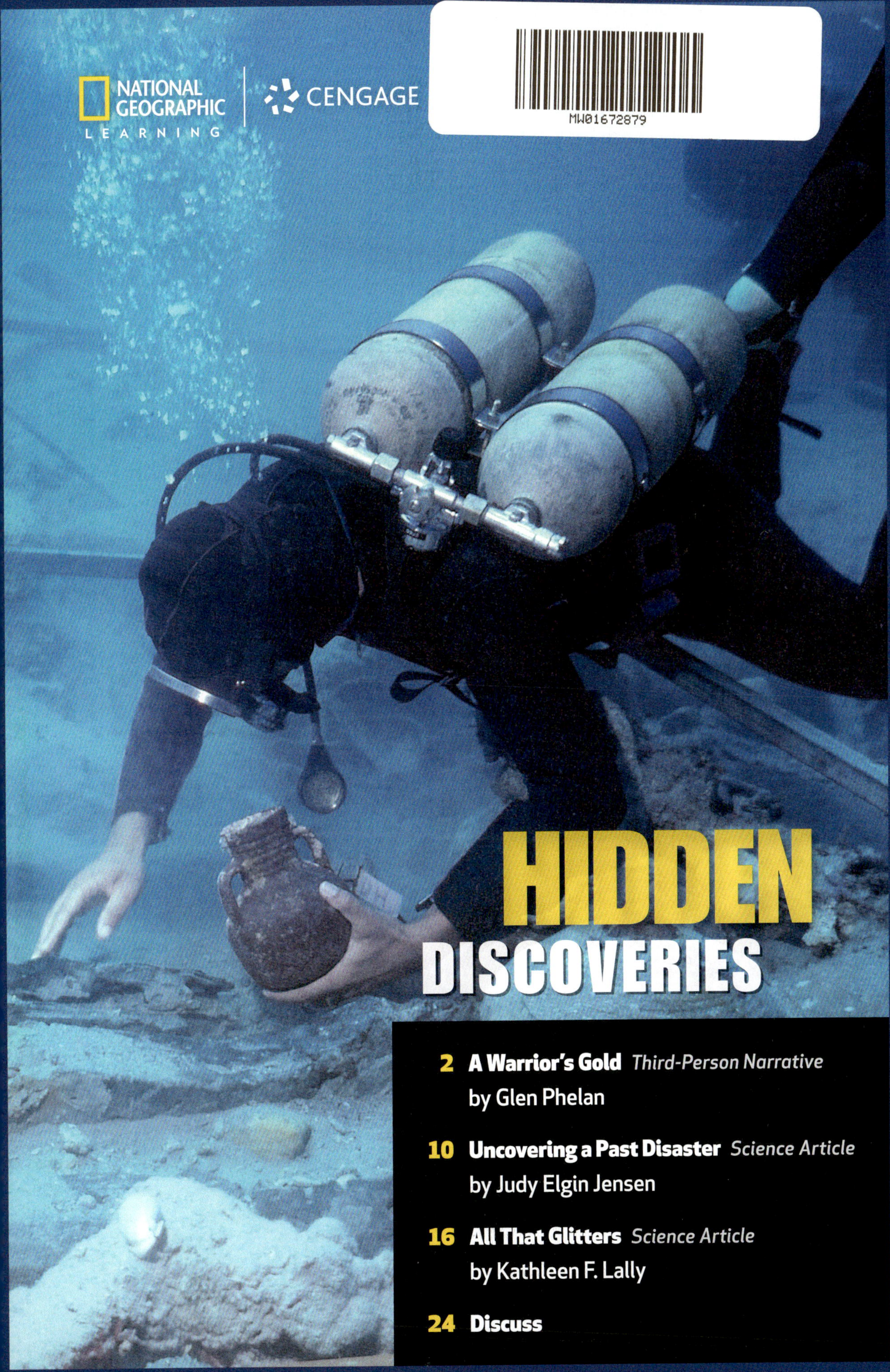

HIDDEN DISCOVERIES

GENRE Third-Person Narrative

Read to find out how magnetic properties helped find artifacts.

A Warrior Gold

by Glen Phelan

The time was the late 600s. A small group of people walked through the English countryside. They were probably warriors. They climbed a small hill. Bushes grew low on the ground. There were dark forests in the distance. The warriors stopped and dug a hole. Then they buried their gold. There it lay hidden until 2009.

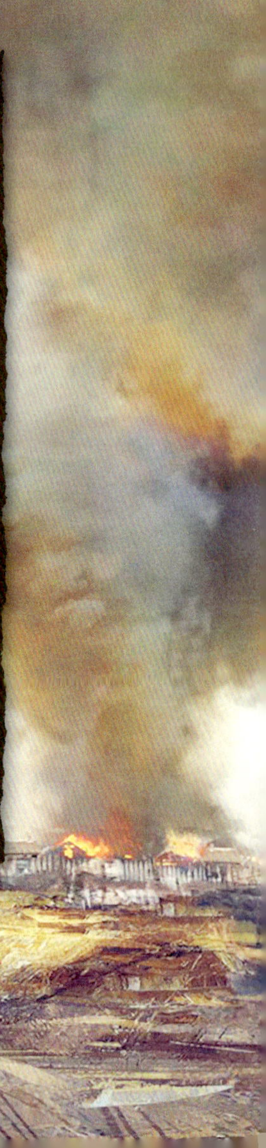

S

The Artifacts Are Found

Terry Herbert walked on that same hill in 2009. He was sweeping a metal detector over the ground. Metal has an unusual **property.** It can become **magnetic** when electricity flows near it. The metal may even be a foot underground. A metal detector uses electricity to make metal objects magnetic. The detector beeps when it picks up a magnetic force. As Terry walked, he heard the sound. *Beep! Beep! Beep!*

A coin placed next to the artifact shows the artifact's size.

Terry didn't know what his detector had found. Maybe some scrap metal or a few old coins. What he dug up was the warrior's gold. Terry was thrilled! He knew that this was a big discovery. It was important to be responsible. Terry told people in charge of the area about his discovery. These people asked archeologists to take a look. Archeologists are scientists who study ancient objects.

Terry Herbert wears gloves to keep dirt and oil from his hands off the artifacts.

The Staffordshire Hoard

This was one of the largest hoards ever discovered. Terry told the right people about his find. That helped archeologists dig up more than 3,500 pieces. The discovery was made in Staffordshire, England. So they called the find the Staffordshire Hoard.

> This piece attached to the helmet. It protected the soldiers face. Pure gold is a fairly soft metal. Mixing gold with other metals makes it stronger.

Most of the objects from the hoard are gold. The hoard is worth more than $5 million. That's interesting. But something else about the find is even more interesting to archeologists.

Nearly every object from the hoard is something used by the military. That's odd. Most discoveries include coins or jewelry. Not this one. It included sword hilts, helmets, and other battle items. What's even more strange? The sword blades are missing. Many of the battle items are bent or broken, too. They seem to have been ruined on purpose.

This golden band is part of the sword's hilt.

What the Hoard Means

People often buried gold to keep it safe. They may have hoped to return for it. The buried gold may have been a religious offering.

Researchers try to figure out why these objects were buried. Some think the gear belonged to an army that lost a battle.

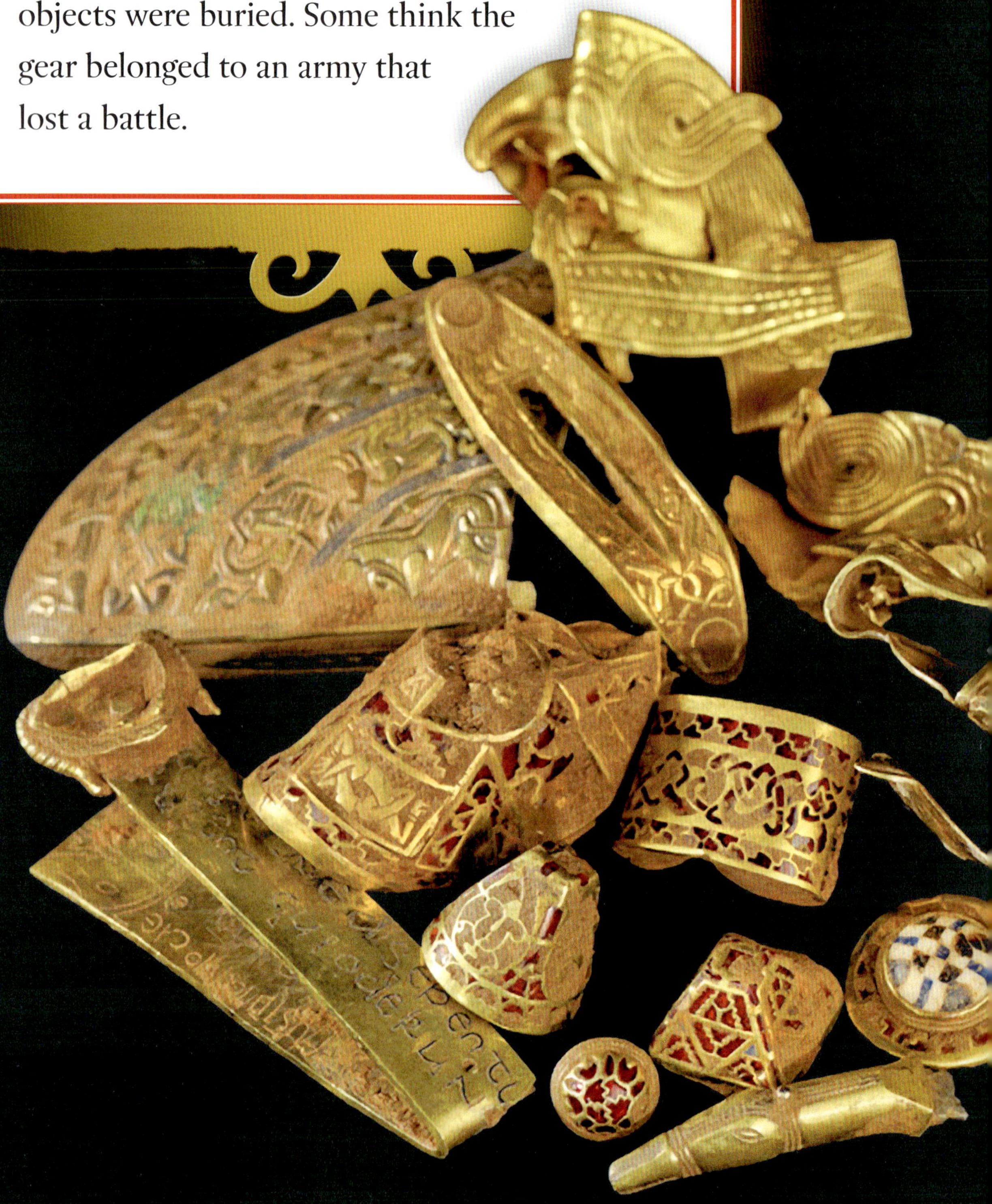

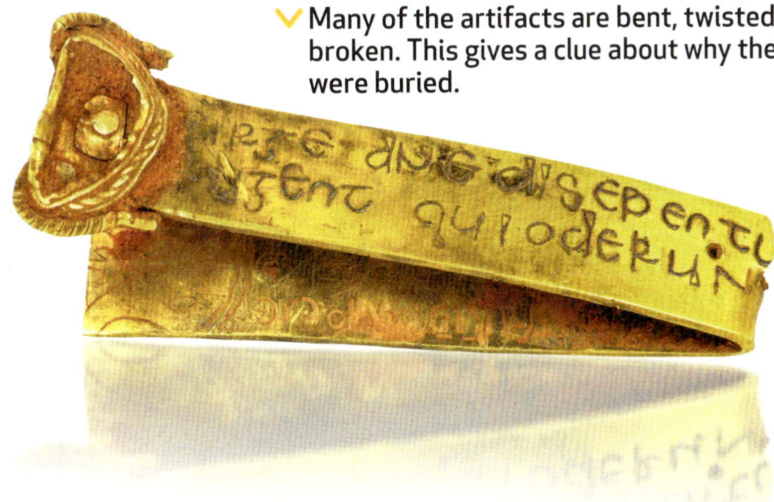

Many of the artifacts are bent, twisted, or broken. This gives a clue about why they were buried.

But why are the pieces bent or broken? In the 7th century, people thought gold was magical. They thought gold protected its owner. They bent and broke the gold to "kill" this property. Then it would not protect enemies who found it.

This is just one idea of who buried the weapons and why. Archaeologists will learn more as they study the Staffordshire Hoard. Then maybe we'll know the full story.

The designs are very detailed. So goldsmiths must have worked very hard on them.

Check In How was Terry able to separate the mixture of gold and soil?

GENRE Science Article

Read to find out how a mixture gave clues to the cause of a disaster.

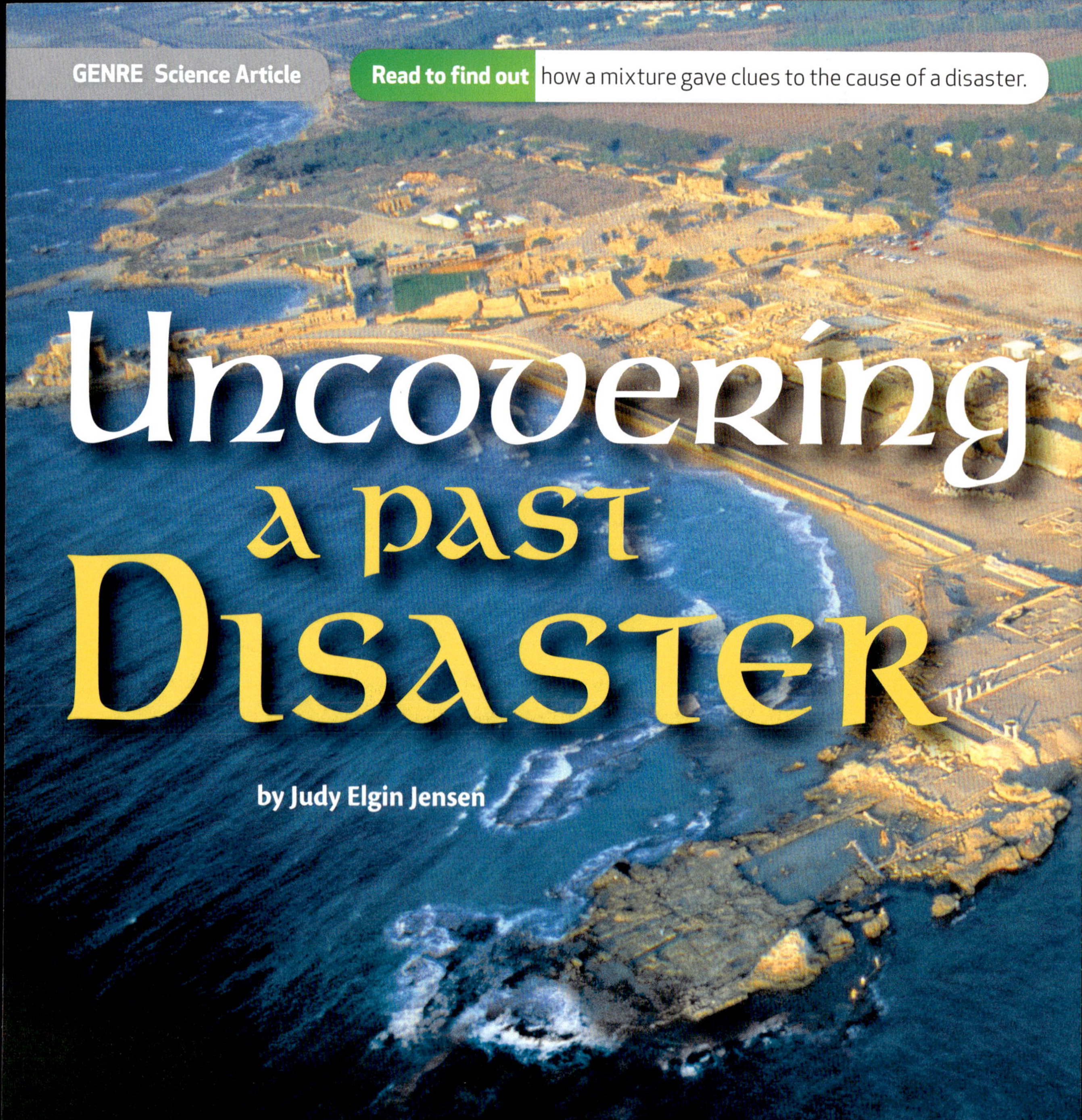

Uncovering a Past Disaster

by Judy Elgin Jensen

Not all discoveries sparkle or shine. Some are special for a different reason. They tell us about past events. Two thousand years ago, Caesarea was an old Roman city. It was a special place. The city had the largest harbor on the eastern coast of the Mediterranean Sea.

Then disaster struck. Written records say a giant wave ruined the harbor. Did that really happen? No one knew for sure until now.

NATIONAL GEOGRAPHIC | EXPLORER

BEVERLY GOODMAN is a geo-archaeologist. She explores seacoasts. She finds clues about natural events that happened in the past. She learns how these events affected people in the past. She then predicts how similar events might affect people today.

Caesarea is located in present-day Israel.

Answers in a Tube

Dr. Goodman is part of a team. The team is collecting core samples at Caesarea. First, they pound a tube into the seafloor. Then it is pulled up. Layers of sand and gravel collect inside the tube. These layers of **sediments** have collected on the seafloor for hundreds or thousands of years. The **mixture** of sediments holds clues about the past.

Dr. Goodman dives to the seafloor with the tube used to get the core sample.

Dr. Goodman was studying a core sample. She saw a layer of shells. Tests showed the age of the shells. They came from the time the harbor was destroyed.

Shells are often found in core samples. They are part of the sediment on the seafloor. A shell layer is usually as thin as your finger. This shell layer was almost 1 meter (3 feet) thick! Most of the shells were broken.

The whole tube, with the sediments inside, is sliced in half.

Shells Tell the Tale

The thick layer of broken shells told Dr. Goodman a story. A giant wave did destroy the harbor. But what really happened?

Here's what Dr. Goodman thinks. An earthquake struck north of Caesarea. Moving rock from the earthquake caused a **tsunami.** This giant wave kicked up shells. The tsunami smashed the shells on the seafloor. Then, the wave crashed into the harbor.

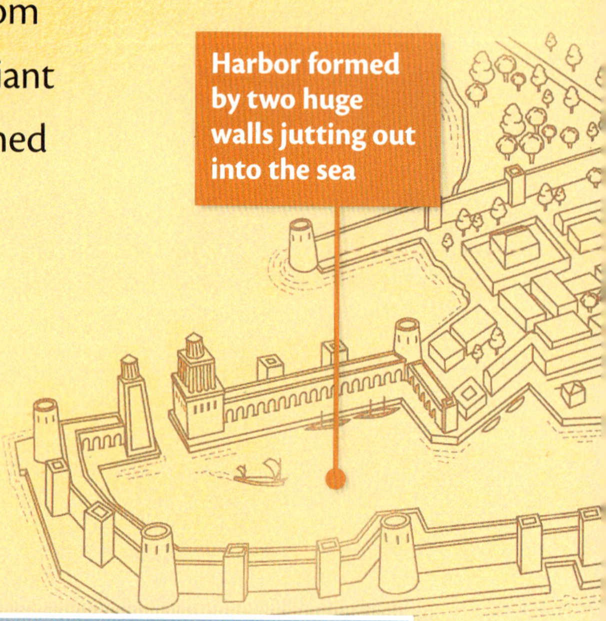

In the past, the hippodrome was used for sporting events. People today still visit it.

Dr. Goodman is planning to study other ancient tsunamis. This will help her predict where future tsunamis will strike. Then people can stop building in those areas.

The amphitheater is still used today for shows.

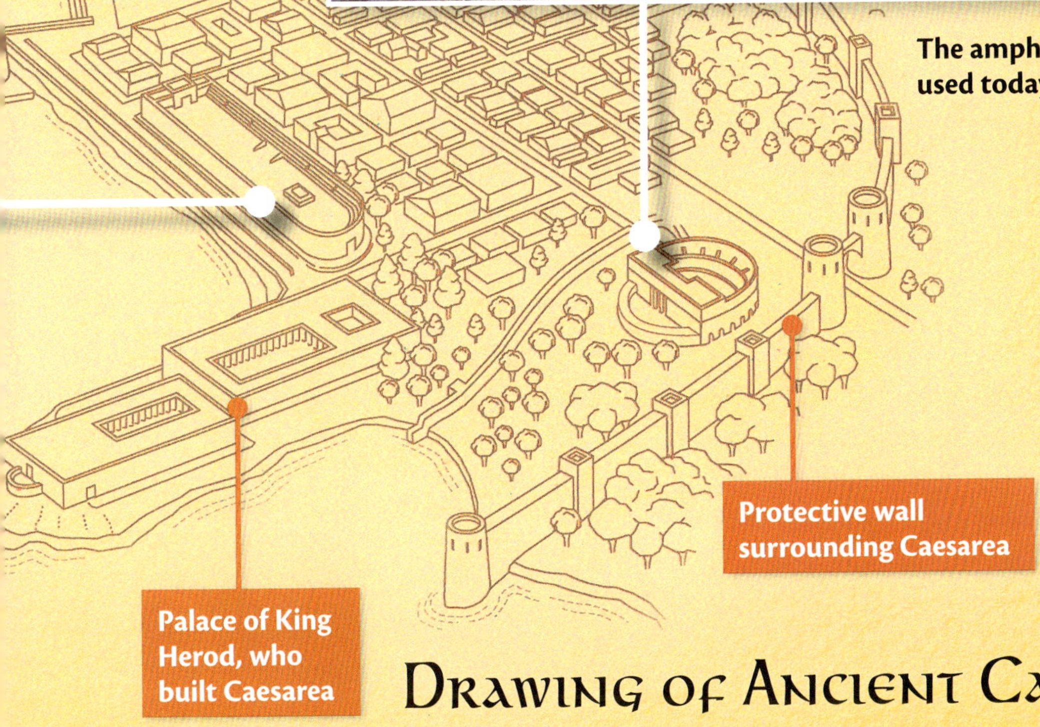

Drawing of Ancient Caesarea

Check In What clues did the layer of shells provide Dr. Goodman about how the ancient harbor of Caesarea was destroyed?

GENRE Science Article

Read to find out how precious stones are mixed in soil.

All That Glitters

by Kathleen F. Lally

Gold! Many people were dreaming about gold in the late 1800s. Someone had found gold nuggets along a river in Canada. The river was near the U.S. state of Alaska. After that, thousands of people rushed there. They came from around the world. A gold rush was on!

Gold prospector in 1899 Alaska

People today can still pan for gold in rivers and streams.

Search for Gold

Miners scooped gravel and sand from the river into shallow pans. They were looking for gold in the sandy **mixture.** Miners held the pans below water level. They gently swirled the mixture. The water washed away the sand and gravel. Bits of stone and gold stayed in the pan. Miners picked the gold from the mixture.

What makes gold so precious? Gold is rare. It also has special **properties,** or qualities. One of these properties is its yellow color. Gold can also be polished and shaped.

Rough opals hint at their beauty.

You can see raw opal in the rocky mixture.

Polishing brings out opals' different colors.

Opal's brilliant sparkle makes it treasured jewelry.

Search for Jade

Now let's go jade hunting. We're headed for Big Sur, California. You can find jade in rocks on the ocean floor. You can also find jade in the mixture of pebbles on the beaches. Jade does not sparkle like opal. It is mostly dull green. Jade can be light green, blue, and black near the water. Jade can also be found in the nearby cliffs. Iron in the soil can turn jade yellow, orange, or red.

Jade Cove, Big Sur, California

If you have trouble finding jade, just wait a bit. The waves turn over the mixture of rocks. Low tide is perfect for jade hunting. The rocks are still wet. That can make it easier to find jade in the rocky mixture.

Jade looks shiny when it's wet.

Unpolished jade stones feel rough.

Jade is very strong. It doesn't break easily. So artists can carve it into delicate shapes.

Search for Diamonds

Would you like to hunt for diamonds? Let's visit Crater of Diamonds State Park in Arkansas. You can dig in an ancient volcanic crater. This volcano reached deep underground to where diamonds form. That's very rare! When the volcano erupted, diamonds rose to the surface. The volcano eroded away long ago. The diamonds haven't. Diamonds are very hard.

Diamonds are hard to find in the soil mixture. Most diamonds are no bigger than the tip of a pen. Plus, rough diamonds don't sparkle. They look like metal and may feel oily. Cut diamonds bend light into a rainbow of color.

Only one perfect diamond has ever been found. Shirley Strawn found it in this park in 1990. It is on display in the visitor center.

A perfect diamond is very rare. Most jewelers have never seen one.

Check In What are some mixtures in which you might find gold, jade, opals, and diamonds?

Discuss

1. How does the title *Hidden Discoveries* connect the three pieces?

2. Compare and contrast the ways in which the discoveries in "A Warrior's Gold" and "Uncovering a Past Disaster" were made.

3. Describe three ways people can separate precious materials from the mixtures in which they are found.

4. Cite some evidence in "Uncovering a Past Disaster" that would confirm that the energy from the tsunami caused the harbor's destruction.

5. What surprised you about the discoveries in this book?